The Ghost of Battle Ridge

by
Susan La Serna
with illustrations by Korah Guilar

Warren Publishing, Inc.

Copyright © 2015
Susan La Serna

All rights reserved. No part of this publication may be reproduced, stored in a retrieval system, or transmitted in any form or any other means electronic, mechanical, photocopying, recording or otherwise, without the prior written permission of the publisher.

Published by Warren Publishing, Inc.
Charlotte, NC
www.warrenpublishing.net

ISBN: 978-1-943258-05-5

Library of Congress Control Number: 2015939012

Published by Warren Publishing, Inc.
www.warrenpublishing.net

Back cover map by Richard Harvey
"Guilford Court House Battleground 1781"
Courtesy of wikipedia.org

Dedication

To my rambunctious grandchildren whose love of adventure and inquiry inspired me to write. And in fond memory of my Siberian Husky whose mischievous antics brought the story to life.

Prologue

    The rumble of cannon fire echoed across the patch of woods as the young soldier staggered over a split rail fence toward a fallen tree trunk. Wounded and desperate, private Mathias S. Mullen of the North Carolina Second Regiment clutched the pendant entangled on his haversack. The tiny portrait of his beloved Kizzy, scorched and misshapen, still dangled from his neck. This battle was over but the cries of the wounded drifted into the evening. Heavy clouds darkened the sky. The stench of gunpowder stung the soldier's eyes and cloaked the forest like a blanket of fog. As he reached for his canteen, great drops of rain began to pour from the sky. Private Mathias Sabbath Mullen was drenched and cold, and his boots were quickly filling with mud. With heavy steps, the wounded soldier sought shelter from the storm, finally huddling inside a burned and hollowed oak tree as the plaintive howl of a lone wolf soared across the river's ridge.

Summer Storm

"Mom! When are we going to be there?"

Mike Agosto was anxious to move to his new home in North Carolina, a far cry from sunny California. The car ride took five days riveting across Highway 40. Now they were just minutes from his new home.

Suddenly, a summer storm rumbled across the Piedmont like cannon fire. Mike had never seen, much less heard, the sounds of summer quite like this. The dark clouds descended upon them like a cloak, and it sent an eerie shiver down his neck as he tried to listen to his iPod.

Curled up on a pile of blankets in the back of their Jeep was Mike's Siberian Husky, Hot Shot. With slanted blue eyes and a silver and white coat, Hot Shot looked like a timber wolf. He was always into mischief, yet loyal to his family. Hot Shot seldom barked, but on occasion would let out the most chilling howl to defend his pack – the Agosto family.

"Hang in there, son," Mike's mom sighed, glancing at her GPS. "As soon as we cross the Haw River, we should be there." Looking worried, she added, "I hope your dad can manage the moving van through this storm." Just then, there was a flash and crackle as a pine branch crashed in front of the Jeep. Hail and wind encompassed the Jeep, causing it to stall on the bridge. Throwing off his ear phones, Mike pressed his face to the car window, watching the river rise and flow under the bridge. Clearly alarmed, Mike's mom looked around for the moving van but found nothing; they were alone on the road. Cautiously, they moved the branch to the side of the road while Hot Shot guarded the family car.

Mike's mom laughed nervously as they drove over debris. "Good thing we have four-wheel drive!" Then, just as suddenly as the storm came, it went. Hot Shot let out a plaintive howl as they drove past the river's ridge to their new home.

Sweet Tea

"This house is awesome! It has such a big yard and no fences." Mike had never seen such a large lot. All the houses in his old neighborhood were practically side by side.

His mother chuckled, "Yeah, it's nice to look out my kitchen window without bumping into my next door neighbor. Be sure to set up your room before your dad gets here."

"Ah, man!" Mike complained.

"What was that?"

"Yes, Mom."

Mike was looking forward to the fifth grade because he could study

US history, his favorite subject. His dad was a history professor whose career was bringing them to UNC Greensboro, and his mom was a veterinarian. Mike was a little like them both; he loved dogs and he loved to read about battles.

Just then, Hot Shot took off to the neighbor's yard. The house had no fence, so Mike could not contain the dog. Lucky for Mike, the neighbor had a dog, too. Hot Shot was playing his own game of crazy eights with a big, brown lab. He loved to run in a figure eight across the yard with anyone who would give chase. This dog was just the challenge Hot Shot needed. Suddenly, the big lab entered her house through the doggie door, and Hot Shot raced in right behind her.

"Oh, no!" Mike cried.

The owners were not home. There was no telling what chaos Hot Shot could make in a stranger's house. Mike ran back to tell his mom what had happened, just as the owners pulled up in their driveway. Frantic, Mike watched from his front porch. A girl about Mike's age got out of the SUV with her mom. The big, brown mutt ran out the doggie door to greet her. Mike couldn't see much else, because the SUV blocked most of his view.

Heart pounding, Mike went into the house to tell his mom. *My mom's a veterinarian*, he thought. *Maybe she can smooth things over with the new neighbors. Let's say, free doggie checkups forever!* Mike desperately called for his mom just as the doorbell rang. Too late! The girl, with her long, wavy auburn hair and bright eyes, was at his door. *Oh, no!* Mike thought, slowly opening the door. The girl handed him a basket of baked goodies.

"Hey," she smiled. "I'm y'alls neighbor. My name is Cora."

"Hi, I'm Mike . . ." Just then the big, brown lab showed up on the doorstep.

"Oh, this is my dog. Her name is Sweet Tea," smiled Cora, gently petting her dog.

"Nice dog," Mike managed to stammer. "I have a dog too, his name is…"

Hot Shot picked that moment to show up on the porch with a slobbery baby doll in his mouth.

Astounded, Cora exclaimed, "Well, bless your heart. That's my doll!"

Hot Shot dropped the doll at Sweet Tea's paws. "Yeah," Mike sighed,

"Hot Shot has a way with the ladies."

Patch of Woods

"*North Cakalak*i is certainly *hecka* greener than *NorCal*, but boy is it humid!" gasped Mike, trying to impress Cora with his cool California slang.

Cora looked puzzled. "Y'all talk too fast, Mike! I didn't understand a thing you said."

"You guys talk too slow, Cora." Mike grinned.

"Well, if you mean North Carolina," said Cora, "It is green because it rains so much in the summer. We get hurricanes, too."

Mike boasted, "In NorCal – I mean, Northern California – we get brush fires because of the hot, dry weather. Plus, there is always a possibility of an earthquake."

Fanning her face, Cora replied, "Listen, if y'all wait, I'll get Sweet Tea and we can go for a walk in the woods near the creek. It's cooler there."

"Sure."

"Great, I'll be right quick."

Sweet Tea and Hot Shot were pals from day one – even if Hot Shot had managed to mangle Cora's baby doll and bury her lip gloss in her front yard. Sweet Tea didn't walk on a leash; she was loyal and obedient. All big, brown eyes and floppy ears, Sweet Tea loved to roam the patch of woods and swim in the rivers and creeks. In contrast, Hot Shot walked with a harness to keep him from pulling Mike through the woods. He was independent and loved to run. If unleashed, there was no telling where he would roam. Hot Shot had powerful endurance, but the heat and humidity were too much for the Siberian Husky. He hated swimming, but he loved the snow. Mike's family used to spend winters in the Sierra Nevada Mountains, where Hot Shot would go sledding with Mike.

"Cora!" exclaimed Mike. "This place is *hecka* cool! It feels much cooler than in our neighborhood."

The woods were mostly deciduous trees; dogwoods, hickory and oak. A few scrappy longleaf pines and hemlock also sprinkled the forest. A granite bolder jutted out, overlooking the creek. Sweet Tea ran to the edge and leapt into the water.

"She loves it here and so do I!" exclaimed Cora.

"I can see why," admired Mike. "It is peaceful."

"It wasn't always so peaceful." Cora said, looking out over the water.

"A fierce battle was fought right here in these woods about 230 years ago."

Cora sighed and poked at a grey anole that was sunbathing on a rock. The anole hissed and expanded its gills, looking like a miniature dinosaur, before turning green and scampering off into the woods.

As the kids talked, Hot Shot lay down on the soft soil with his forepaws and hindquarters splayed like a bear rug.

"Why does he lay like that, Mike?"

"Huskies cool themselves by laying their bellies in the soft soil."

"Why doesn't he just swim in the creek like Sweet Tea?"

"I don't know, but wait until winter. He is magnificent in the snow."

School Daze

Summer was ending. Soon school would start. Mike didn't just like school; he loved it. He was a good student and rarely got into trouble. He and Cora were in Mrs. Nash's fifth grade class. Mike couldn't wait.

Mike gathered his backpack full of school supplies and headed for the bus stop. He was always nervous on the first day of school. Today, he was especially anxious because he didn't know anyone but Cora. The bus ride was long, crowded and noisy. It seemed to go down every country road in the Triad. The potholes in the road rattled the old bus and made everyone jiggle and bounce in their seats. Pine branches scraped the windows and threatened to clutch the daylights out of unwary, sleepy students. Finally, the bus arrived at the loop, where the students had to sit and wait until the bell rang.

Cora got off the bus ahead of Mike, but acted like she was fixing her shoes so that he could catch up.

Once they were together, Mike started talking excitedly until a teacher sternly said, "Young man, mind your manners and use your inside voice." Mike looked down, silently walking alongside Cora.

Finally, they were down the fifth grade hall, standing outside Mrs. Nash's room. She came to the door and greeted everyone as she gave them a seat assignment and group number. Cora sat in group two. Mike sat in group five.

Mrs. Nash was neither young nor old. She had straight dark hair and wore glasses. She looked strict, especially when she folded her arms and raised one eyebrow. But she had a gentle smile. Strict but fair. Mike could live with that.

Most of the students in his group knew each other. Mike felt a bit left out. He missed his buddies in California. He slung his backpack under his desk and all his school supplies tumbled across the floor. Mrs. Nash raised one eyebrow, then folded her arms. *Oh no*, thought Mike, *not the teacher look!* Nervously, he got up to gather his things but the pencils kept scattering across the floor.

Mrs. Nash briskly said, "Mike, put your bookbag in your cubby *right quick.*"

Still looking down, Mike could feel his face burning with embarrassment. Feeling confused, he mistakenly wondered why the teacher wanted him to put his books in a bag. He quickly got his books out of his desk and looked to see if he had a bag in his cubby. Now the students in his group started to snicker and giggle. This day was a disaster.

Mrs. Nash paused and lowered her voice.

"Young man. What are you doing?"

"Putting my books in a bag?" questioned Mike.

Now everyone laughed except Cora. Mike thought to himself, *teachers speak differently in California. The school rules are different in California. I wish I was in California!*

Mrs. Nash thought that Mike was acting like the class clown and she would not tolerate it, and Mike didn't realize that a backpack was called a bookbag in North Carolina. He honestly, but mistakenly, thought Mrs. Nash wanted him to put his books in a bag.

Tapping her foot rapidly, arms folded, and one eyebrow raised, Mrs.

Nash tersely exclaimed, "Are you acting the fool, Mike?"

Mike never acted up in class, not even for substitute teachers. He was appalled that the teacher would think that he was misbehaving.

Emphatically, he exclaimed "No!"

Eyebrow still raised, Mrs. Nash said, "No… what?"

Confused and embarrassed, Mike repeated, "No, I'm not."

Still tapping her foot, Mrs. Nash glared at Mike. He did not know what she wanted him to say. In California, students didn't speak as formally as they do in North Carolina. If only he knew the rules.

Cora was whispering loudly from her group, "No, Ma'am. Say, 'No Ma'am'."

Poor Mike couldn't make out what Cora or the teacher wanted. It sounded like Cora was saying, "Oh, man! Say, 'Oh, man!'"

Finally, Mrs. Nash looked at Mike and Cora and said, "You two just earned silent lunch."

"Yes, *Ma'am*," sighed Cora McQuillan as she quickly cast Mike a sympathetic glance.

Gooder'n Grits

Mike and Cora had silent lunch but not silent lunch line. The menu was barbeque, slaw, and a choice of hush puppies or leftover breakfast grits. Mike expected barbeque to be a grilled piece of meat smothered with a savory red sauce. Not so in North Carolina. He stared down at a hamburger bun filled with shredded mystery meat!

"Where's the barbeque?" Mike exclaimed.

The lunch lady scowled. "On your plate!"

Cora whispered, "It's inside your bun."

Mike was even more confused. Next, the lunch lady handed him vinegar sauce to spritz onto his mystery meat. Clearly irritated, the lunch

lady asked, "Grits or hush puppies?"

Mike had never eaten either, so he replied, "I guess I'll try a grit." Rolling her eyes, she slopped a scoopful of white mush onto Mike's plate.

Returning to their silent lunch table, Mike began to eat his mystery meat with the vinegar sauce. To his amazement, it was the most tender shredded pork he had ever tasted. The vinegar sauce made the pork melt in his mouth. He had no problem with silent lunch because his mouth was stuffed full with barbeque pork on a bun!

Talking with his mouth full, Mike exclaimed, "Wow! This is good stuff! I mean, it's *really* good stuff!"

"Yeah," whispered Cora. "The secret's in the vinegar sauce."

Poking at his plate, Mike mumbled, "But I think she forgot to give me my grit."

"It isn't one grit, silly. It's grits." Cora pointed. "It's the white mush on your tray."

Surprised, Mike said, "Oh! My mom makes this out of yellow corn meal. We call it polenta."

"Is it good?" asked Cora.

"Gooder'n grits!" winked Mike.

Eye of the Storm

"It's not the heat, it's the humidity!" Mike gasped as the barometer continued to drop. The weather was insufferable. Mike was used to clear-skied California summers with triple digit heat, but he was not used to this Carolina humidity. Even Mrs. Nash would not allow the students to go outdoors.

A Category 4 hurricane had been looming off the Atlantic coast for several days. Cora was tracking the possible trajectory it would take on her storm tracker worksheet. Cora was a math whiz. She could turn any assignment into a math problem. According to Cora's predictions, the hurricane should hit the shore in less than three hours. The clouds were so low and heavy it looked as though you could touch them, and they darkened the sky so much that the street lights turned on. Then, an announcement came across the school intercom:

"Impending storm! School dismissal!"

The hurricane was picking up speed, causing severe wind gusts and lightning strikes. The students let out a cheer. Mike wasn't as thrilled. He was worried about Hot Shot. Hot Shot was an outdoor dog. Mike and his dad made Hot Shot a secure dog house and kennel, but Mike would feel much better as soon as his whole family was home, safe and sound.

Dismissal was crazy. The car pool loop was packed with anxious parents trying to get their children safely home. Mike's mom wanted to pick him up, but she had an emergency surgery on an injured animal. His dad was away at a conference. Mike would have to take the bus home and put Hot Shot inside the house. Taking a deep breath, Mike thought, *I can do this.*

The bus ride was shaky as the winds worsened. The rumble of thunder vibrated across the Piedmont. Lightning illuminated the otherwise dark skies, and an eerie greenish hue hovered over the horizon. At last, the bus arrived at his house. Mike raced to get Hot Shot. To his horror, the dog was gone. He had dug under the kennel and escaped. The pit of Mike's stomach ached as he worried about Hot Shot in this storm. He called his mom's office and left an urgent message. His mom had microchipped Hotshot with their name and address, precisely in the event of a moment like this. Still, Mike could not shake the worry from his mind. Pacing his room, Mike watched as the snap and crash of tree limbs echoed across the patch of woods. The horizon sizzled a metallic green as transformers and cable lines blew out. Mike thought most of the region must be without electricity by now. He decided to go out and search for Hot Shot.

Mrs. McQuillan, Cora's mother, looked out her window and saw Mike leaving. Beckoning to him, she calmly said, "Sweetie, your mom called me. It is too dangerous for her to travel. You are staying with us until this storm passes." Relieved, Mike told her about his dog. He wanted to cry, but didn't dare shed a tear in front of Cora. Just then, Sweet Tea put her head on Mike's lap and let out a soft whimper. She was worried, too.

Toublesome Creek

The hurricane made landfall with a fury, dumping flood waters across the coastal plains and ripping up tree limbs inland. The trees were strewn across the roads like scattered toothpicks. Then, out of nowhere, the skies cleared, the air cooled, and dawn came. The neighborhood was without power, and men gathered the fallen limbs, cutting and trimming them with chainsaws while the women pulled out the grills and had a cookout for everyone. Children helped fill ice chests with soft drinks, and it looked like a block party.

Sensing Mike's anxiety, Mrs. McQuillan allowed Cora and Sweet Tea to help him look for Hot Shot in the woods. She cautioned them to stay clear of the river and swollen creeks. Their patch of woods looked like a battle zone! Branches were strewn around, uprooted tree trunks gnarled the sky, and sludge blanketed the forest. Blue heron, white tailed deer, and foxes scampered about, looking for shelter. Calling frantically for his dog, Mike's voice was lost in the rush of the raging creek.

Suddenly Sweet Tea perked her ears, yelped, and ran in circles around Cora as if to say, "Follow me!"

Racing across the soggy forest floor, Sweet Tea was getting dangerously close to the rising creek. They began to hear faint whimpers and howls.

"Is it Hot Shot?" asked Mike, plodding toward the creek.

Cora grasped his arm and warned, "It's not safe, Mike!"

Mud and debris were piled in the creek, and the mound looked like a beaver dam. Sweet Tea was on a boulder, barking frantically at a tangle of muck and tree limbs wedged against the creekbank. Racing to the edge, Mike and Cora could see a muddy mound moving and heaving inside the slime. Then, two blue eyes pierced through the sludge. It was Hot Shot, and he was a pitiful, tangled mess! Desperately, the kids tried to untangle him, but the swift waters kept pushing him further into the creek. Then, with one final heave, Mike and Cora lifted a fallen limb and Sweet Tea helped drag it to the boulder.

Once released, Hot Shot leapt to the bank, licking and jumping on his owner. Then, with one quick twist, Hot Shot gave himself a good shake, splashing his friends with mud. Mike didn't care; he was so relieved. Hugging his pal, Mike felt a cold, hard object tangled in Hot

Shot's fur. He tugged and grasped at a rectangular metal pendant the size of a postage stamp. Curious, he wiped the mud from it with his sleeve. Faintly visible was a miniature portrait of a young woman. The metal edge of the pendant was mangled and distorted, and a tiny piece of blackened leather was twisted onto the clasp.

"What did this troublesome creek unearth?" asked Mike as he fingered the strange object. His Husky cast an inquisitive look with his piercing blue eyes, as if to say, "Time will tell."

Brown-Eyed Maiden

Professor Agosto carefully cleaned the tiny pendant, holding it in his hand as though it was a delicate butterfly wing. The pendant was a miniature watercolor portrait of a colonial maiden wearing a white lace mob cap tied at the chin with dark blue ribbon. She was dressed in a pale blue sack gown fitted at the waist with a v-shaped stomacher. Her sleeves, trimmed in ivory lace, contrasted gently with her soft bronze skin. The background of the miniature was painted in pale yellow and sepia and encased in enamel. A small scorch with a string of flecks along the edges of the tiny portrait was the only sign of damage. Fragmented pieces of the braided leather chain were still attached to the pendant.

"It looks like a mourning pendant," remarked Professor Agosto. "It was popular in Colonial times to carry a pendant of a deceased loved one, although they usually contained a locket of hair." Mike's dad was using a magnifying glass to make out the details. Turning the pendant over and over, he continued, "However, it could also be a love locket. It's really hard to say. The blue ribbon on her mob cap may suggest that she was married." On the back of the gilded metal pendant was the inscription, B'lvd Keziah LaSante 1774. "This is quite a find, son," Professor Agosto said as he removed his glasses.

Mike couldn't wait to search the archives and records of the colonial era. His dad had access to most of the primary documents in the University libraries. Mike was no stranger to research; he practically grew up in the card catalog. He couldn't wait to go to UNC Greensboro with his dad. Cora, on the other hand, hated history and would rather be doing a Sudoku math puzzle. This tiny portrait, however, caught her interest as she pondered the fate of this mysterious brown-eyed maiden.

"This belongs in a museum," Cora mused.

Join or Die

Mrs. Nash assigned group history projects on the Southern Campaign of the Revolutionary War. Each group had to select a banner or flag to represent the Patriots from the years 1776-1781. The students also had to pick a job or trade to represent the era.

"Mike, Matthew, Cora, Mikayla and Santiago," called Mrs. Nash. "Your group is assigned the Battle of Guilford Court House. The year is 1781."

Mikayla was excited to be with Cora. "Let's make a flag with a crown on it! I think it should have glitter, too," she suggested.

"You can't do that," moaned Matthew. "We are Patriots, not Loyalists." "I think we should have a snake!" suggested Santiago.

"Ewww," snapped Cora. "That's gross."

"Not really," remarked Mike. "The snake logo was quite common in the Revolutionary Period. Even Benjamin Franklin designed one. Here, look." Mike pointed to the book with a picture of a black and white flag of a dismembered snake. Underneath were the names of the original colonies, and in bold letters were the words, "Join or Die."

"That's not a flag. That's a cartographic map!" Cora exclaimed.

"*A carta-what?*" Santiago asked, reaching for the book to get a better look.

Cora was excited now. "A cartograph! It's a flag made in the likeness of a map. See how the snake curves in the shape of the Atlantic coastline."

"Ah, cool!" marveled Santiago. "Look! The snake's head is New England. Then, it curves until the tail ends in South Carolina."

Mikayla grabbed the book. "Maybe we could make our flag with a crown on the snake's head." Mikayla loved fashion and jewelry. If they were to design a flag, it would be stylish!

Matthew sighed, frustrated with Mikayla. "The crown represents King George III."

Then, Santiago exclaimed, "I vote we give our snake fangs!"

"Gross! I'm still not voting for any fangs," pouted Cora, folding her arms in disgust.

"Why, not?" Mikayla, asked. "Vampires have fangs, and I love vampire books."

Matthew rolled his eyes. "Great. Here we go again with the girly *Midnight* books."

"Not *Midnight*, silly. It's *Twilight*. And they're not girly. Even Mrs. Nash reads them!" Mikayla blushed. She thought Matthew was quite adorable in his ignorance.

Cora and Santiago looked at each other and shook their heads. They were both thinking the same thing. *Those two argue like an old married couple.*

Finally, Cora shrugged her shoulders and voted for the snake flag.

Mike could not wait to do the project. He eagerly announced, "Then it's settled. Join or Die!"

High Road to Salisbury

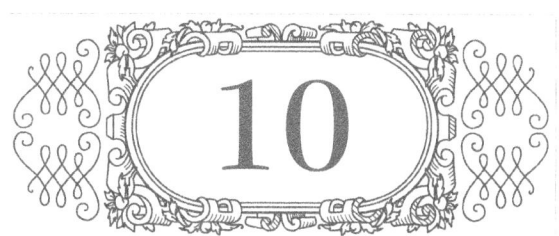

Mike could not wait to do his research, but Cora moaned at the thought of researching things that had already happened. She preferred math and science. Nonetheless, the pendant that they found of the lovely colonial maiden lingered in Cora's thoughts. *Was Keziah's life that different than mine?* Only time could answer that question.

Mikayla was thrilled to research the clothes and styles of the colonial days. She begged Mike to let her look at the pendant of Keziah LaSante. "Well, my dad has it. His colleagues are testing it for authenticity at UNC Chapel Hill."

Excited, Matthew asked, "Ooh – could we do our research at Carolina?"

"I think that can be arranged," Mike replied with a grin.

The little group met at Mike's house that weekend, and Dr. Agosto piled the chatty group into her Jeep for the hour-long trip to the Research Triangle.

Leaving Greensboro, Santiago shouted, "Look! The High Road to Salisbury. That's where the Patriots fought the British at the Battle of Guilford Court House." Lowering his voice, Santiago continued, "Did you know that General Cornwallis fired on his own soldiers just to win the battle?"

"That's just plain wrong. It makes me ill to think about it," Cora said.

Looking down, she pondered, "I wonder what side Keziah LaSante was on?"

"Either way," continued Santiago, "about 200 men died and there were too many wounded or missing to count."

"Yeah," sighed Matthew. "Cornwallis ordered his officers to fire cannons and grapeshot into the battle. They sprayed grape-sized metal balls everywhere, wounding more of their own men than the Patriots'."

Mike spoke up. "Even Cornwallis' saddle caught on fire and His Majesty's guards had to tamp it out to save the General."

Dr. Agosto just shook her head. "That poor horse!"

As they continued on their journey to Chapel Hill, the children all looked mournfully back at their home town. It was just like looking back in time.

Milliner's Daughter

"Marry me, dearest Keziah." The young officer looked dashing in his crisp red coat and white breeches. Playfully, he stretched down on bended knee with his hand held on his heart.

Keziah demurred as she straightened the bolts of the latest floral cotton chintz fabric shipped from London. "Perchance do you mock me,

Major Nolan? Who shall tend my shop?"

"Keziah, once my service at Fort Johnson is complete, we can build our life in London. You will wear only the finest gowns. Besides, Royal Governor Josiah Martin will not tolerate much more insolence from these rebellious colonists."

Keziah agreed. "Can you ever imagine tossing all that tea into the Boston Harbor? All because of a half-penny tax? I should hope the same does not happen in New Bern." Lowering her voice, she added, "I do hear murmurings from the ladies of Edenton. They have signed a petition to boycott tea and British goods. To think, Lady Penelope signed! And my best customer, too! What shall we do without goods from England? Mother and I depend on the latest fabrics from England to fill our milliner's shop."

Just then, the tiny bell on the shop door chimed as one of New Bern's finest ladies entered.

"Good day, Mistress Keziah. Perchance is my Polonaise gown ready?"

"Most certainly, Madame Moseley. My mantua maker and her seamstresses are pinking the final stitches." Keziah beckoned Madame Moseley of Alden Manor to the fitting room.

"Please do come this way."

The Major gently tapped Keziah's hand, whispering, "Dearest Keziah, do me the honor of sitting for a miniature portrait. Lt. Colonel Martin has agreed that his master artisan will do the watercolor. His painter is a renowned enameller who studied under Master Copley."

Curtseying quickly, Keziah put a bonnet on her head and twirled around lightly. "Whatever did you do to deserve his favor?"

"I simply saved his Royal Governor from the tirades of the Regulators!"

Upon leaving, the officer opened the shop door and a grey tabby kitten scurried into the shop. The feline purred softly, dancing around Keziah's dainty ankles. Gently picking up the kitten, Keziah whispered, "Oh

Millie, these are tumultuous times, such tumultuous times indeed!"

Go Heels!

Dr. Agosto parked the Jeep in the South Building parking lot as the kids excitedly tumbled out. Crossing the street, they admired the university's cobblestone pathways, ancient oaks, and colonial brick buildings.

Looking at the plaque on the wall of one of the buildings, Cora exclaimed, "It says here that Old East is the oldest public school building in the United States – it was built in 1793!"

At that moment, Professor Agosto and his colleague, Professor Guilar, met the kids. The children eagerly greeted them. "Just call me Miss Jill," Professor Guilar said, welcoming them to UNC Chapel Hill.

The kids eagerly gathered around the two professors for a mini-history lesson of the University of North Carolina at Chapel Hill.

"William Richardson Davie was a Revolutionary War hero, tenth Governor of North Carolina, and founder of this university!" Professor Agosto remarked. "He and his cavalry fought with Nathanael Greene, aiding them with supplies and food for the military in North Carolina."

"In fact," interjected Miss Jill, "I have a miniature portrait of Mr. Davie in my office in Hamilton Hall. It is very similar to the pendant you found during the storm. Would you like to see it?"

The kids couldn't contain their excitement, replying in unison, "Yes please, Miss Jill!" The little group skipped and jumped along the shady cobblestone paths surrounded by brick buildings with noble columns and stairs.

"Just think," Mike said, awestruck. "We are walking along the same path as William Davie, who helped in the Battle of Guilford Court House!"

"That's right, Mike," added Miss Jill. "Mr. Davie supported Nathanael Greene and helped the Patriots continue in skirmishes from Charlotte to Guilford."

The group stopped in front of the famous Old Well, a water fountain under a neoclassical rotunda with white columns and a powder blue dome.

Professor Agosto explained, "The two colors were chosen in colonial times as a compromise of two rivaling schools. One school's color was sky blue, and the other's was white. This spot was the original water well for the tiny colonial town of Chapel Hill, a town that needed unity, not rivalry."

"Yes," replied Miss Jill. "William Davie wanted the public school and the town to represent all Carolinians of all backgrounds. So they chose their school colors to be both sky blue and white."

"So why do they call themselves Tar Heels?" Santiago asked.

"University students embraced the name Carolina Tar Heels because the British made such fun of the poor barefooted North Carolinians with pine tar on their heels. The university students wear the name with pride!"

Santiago, Mikayla, Matthew, Cora, and Mike each took turns drinking from the fountain as Mike's mom readied the camera.

"Everybody say, 'Go Heels!'"

Phantom Footprints

Mike woke up to the gently falling snow. The early morning snow glistened royal blue and palest white on his window sill.

"Snow day!" he exclaimed.

Although it was a Wednesday, Mike knew school would be closed today. Looking out his window, he could see Hot Shot delightedly curled up in the snowy yard outside his dog house. A brilliant red cardinal sat perched above Hot Shot's dog house, unafraid of the Siberian Husky. The snow was their mutual friend. Mike couldn't wait to put on his snow boots and take Hot Shot for a run in the woods.

Clamoring down the stairs, Mike yelled, "No schooooool!"

Professor Agosto was checking the news to see if his classes at UNC Greensboro would be canceled, too. The family was abuzz with excitement.

"Can I go sledding with Hot Shot?"

"First things first," said Mike's mom. "You need to eat a good breakfast and bundle up. See if any of your friends want to come with you." Mike knew that Cora and Sweet Tea would be awake soon. Perhaps his other schoolmates would want to come along too, especially since they all lived in the same neighborhood.

The phone rang; it was Santiago. He wanted to know if the group would like to go exploring in the woods behind the neighborhood. Mike invited Santiago over so they could get ready. Mikayla had already texted Matthew and they were on their way. Cora's lights were on in her house and Sweet Tea was already playing in the yard with Hot Shot. The gang arrived at Mike's front porch roaring and ready to go.

"I know a place by the river's ridge where we can go sledding," said Mike, pulling on his boots. "It has a small hill and clearing before you reach the ridge."

"Terrific!" exclaimed Santiago. "Let's go!"

Santiago was not used to the snow. He was born in Costa Rica, a tropical country with sandy beaches. He didn't even own a good pair of snow shoes, so he put plastic grocery bags over his shoes.

"*Bless your heart,* Santiago!" giggled Mikayla.

"Are those grocery bags from the Piggly Wiggly?"

"Yeah," Santiago shrugged. "You know what they say... Down home down the street."

"Down the street, not on your feet!" Matthew corrected with a yawn.

The little group knocked on Cora's door as Hot Shot and Sweet Tea readied for the river's ridge.

The children gathered in the clearing and marveled at the pristine view. The open meadow was covered in snow, like icing on a wedding cake.

"It sparkles like a princess forest!" admired Mikayla.

"Sweet!" admitted Matthew.

The meadow was perfectly smooth and white. The ridge above the meadow was covered in icicles, and they shimmered over the hemlock trees and barren oaks like crystal feathers. An eerie silence surrounded them.

The little group stood frozen, as if under a spell, looking at the meadow. A chill wind gusted through the meadow, tossing powdery snow over their heads. Huddling together, the children shielded their faces from the bitter cold. Nipping at their ears, the wind echoed faint whispers. They were wiping the snowflakes from their eyes when suddenly, out of nowhere, phantom footprints appeared on the snowy ground. The kids watched in mystified silence as the steps continued down the meadow toward the river's ridge – except no one was there! They were so frightened, they were too scared to run. The hair on the nape of Hot Shot's neck stiffened as he glided magnificently across the meadow, racing toward the moving footprints. The footprints stopped abruptly on the ridge.

The little group stood in the meadow, mesmerized. Hot Shot sat perched on the ridge, his head tilted high as he howled toward the sky; a long, chilling, and plaintive wail. His howl vibrated and echoed across the meadow, startling birds from the trees and sending them flying toward the heavens. Then, just as mysteriously as the footprints appeared, they vanished! The meadow was once again covered in untouched snow. Stunned, the children looked breathlessly toward the ridge. Without warning, the icicles on the trees began to shake violently, whistling like wind chimes. Then, cascading from the ridge, the icicles landed at the children's feet, spread out like angel's wings.

In unison, the little group whispered, "What just happened?"

Backwoodsman

Keziah slowly arranged the hats in her shop window. Business had been difficult ever since Royal Governor Martin was expelled from Tryon Palace by the Regulators. The Governor had hastened to Fort Johnson on his royal navy sloop in the summer of '75. Keziah had not seen the dashing British Major Nolan in so many years. She looked longingly out her window as Lady Cogwell Stanly walked her little son John to New Bern Academy. It seemed but a mere yesteryear that Master Johnny Stanly was a young boy playing in her shop. The child used to chase after Millie, the kitten, with ribbons while Lady Ana Stanly shopped for fabric to adorn her latest caraco jacket or stylish hat. Keziah LaSante was now a mature, single woman of twenty. The promise of marriage and family was a distant memory. Why, even Millie the cat had a family of her own!

At that precise moment, Millie ran from her perch on the counter and out the door. She was such a curious creature. Keziah suspected that Millie knew more of the colony's goings-on than most folks – and she was smarter than most colonists, too. Oh, the tales Miss Millie could tell.

Just then, the door chimed open and in walked a tall, lanky frontiersman. He clearly belonged in the backcountry, with his buckskin jacket and handsewn leggings. Removing his cap, he stammered bashfully.

"Lassie, I'm alookin' for Jacob Mullen from Perquimans County."

Surprised, Keziah replied, "The Mullen plantation is quite far from here. The British have burned many of the plantations in that region."

"Yes'm. I've been drafted from Yadkin county to substitute for Mr. Mullen as part of the North Carolina Rifle Militia."

Keziah hated what the war was doing to the colonies, and the peril in which it put her family, many of whom were still enslaved on the Moseley plantation. How she wanted this backcountry Minuteman to leave her shop! She loathed the turmoil and bloodshed started by a protest over taxation without representation, representation that Keziah and her family would never see, regardless of the war's outcome.

"Well, sir, I shall not help you, nor do I endorse your cause!"

"My cause, lassie, is for the colonies to be free!"

Placing her hands on her tiny waist and stomping her foot, Keziah's face flushed. "Free? Free? My mother was a seamstress and house slave for William Moseley! Do you know, sir, the price she paid for her freedom?

Most of my family remains in slavery on that plantation!"

The tall backwoodsman looked awkwardly out the window at Millie the cat, who sat up straight, ears twitching at every word her mistress uttered.

"And what about the ladies, eh?" Keziah continued. "Does your cause intend to free the ladies?"

The backwoodsman touched his unshaven chin. He was at a loss for words and unsure how to extricate himself from this argument. His superb hunting skills along the Blue Ridge Mountains and his keen marksmanship were no match for the sharp, fiery tongue of this pretty lass. He had only come into the shop because she caught his eye when arranging straw hats in her shop window. He realized his chances of courting her were now impossible. He wanted to tell her that he was not exactly thrilled about fighting either, that he would rather be hunting in the backcountry along Graveyard Gap with the likes of Daniel Boone and the other frontiersmen. Boiling sinew from deerskins in a kettle to make his own clothes and weapons was what he was best at.

"Well, lassie, I was just fixin' to leave. I'm just a country cousin of Jacob. Name's Mathias Sabbath Mullen, and it's a pleasure to have made your acquaintance." He set his coonskin cap back on his head and bowed slightly.

In spite of herself, Keziah couldn't help notice what a bashfully handsome young fellow Mathias was. With his dark, curly hair, suntanned skin and rugged features, he was quite the opposite of her British Major.

"Well, I suppose you shall buy some soap whilst here. Clearly you haven't bathed in some time!"

"Yes, Lassie, I reckon I'll be needin' a shave, too."

Keziah pointed her delicate bronze arm toward the street. "The barber shop is near Front Street."

"Aye, lass." Mathias backed clumsily into a bolt of fabric, knocking it to the floor. The fabric unraveled at Keziah's feet. Embarrassed, Mathias retrieved it and, after folding it, placed it back on the counter.

Keziah smiled as he ambled toward the barber's shop. Clutching the pendant pinned on her frock, she pondered, *why does my heart flutter so?*

Battle of Guilford Court House

15

Mrs. Nash's class was preparing for their final project on the Southern Campaign, and the students were readying for a multimedia presentation. Mikayla had researched the fabric and clothing of the times, and Matthew had a slide presentation with colonial music and lyrics. Mike and Santiago researched the military details of the final Battle at Guilford Court House, which took place on March 15, 1781. Cora synthesized the project into a cohesive PowerPoint presentation.

The grand finale was the Battle of Guilford Court House reenactment! Revolutionary War reenactors gathered at Tannenbaum and Greensboro Country Park each March for the reenactment. Cora's mom, Mrs.

McQuillan, prepared to take the little group on Saturday to the event at Country Park. Even Hot Shot and Sweet Tea were going. It was a popular event in Greensboro, an occasion for families to have an outing with their leashed dogs to watch the battle reenactors. Tents were set up with colonial items on display and for sale.

"Look at all the street names!" exclaimed Santiago. "There's Cornwallis Street and Liberty. Wow, now I get it! All the names in downtown Greensboro are named from the Revolutionary War."

"The houses on Lawndale Avenue are so old and beautiful!" remarked Mikayla. "Even the tree-lined streets look like they were here three centuries ago!"

"Here we are! Nathanael Greene Country Park," announced Mrs. McQuillan.

"Yeah! Let's go!" exclaimed the group.

"Now, wait just a minute, sweet peas," smiled Mrs. McQuillan. "First we must have a meeting place in case we get separated."

They all agreed to wait by the pond next to the bridge at 4:00 p.m. The little group scrambled to leash the dogs and make it to the park. People everywhere were strolling with their pets. Some were dressed in colonial attire; others were just out for a late winter walk.

Cora had already gotten a map and was surveying the park. "Look here. We can visit different camp sites that are selling their wares, and we can even interview reenactors from both sides of the battle!"

"Why don't we divide into groups and meet at the battle site at 2:00?" Matthew suggested.

"Good idea," replied Mike. "That way we can film and gather all the information that we need for our project."

"Sounds like a plan!" said Mrs. McQuillan.

"Come on," exclaimed Mike. "Let's go!"

Keziah's Prayer

Keziah looked out her millinery shop's window at the pouring rain. She anxiously awaited word from her husband. The long, dreary war was now entering its fifth year. The Committee of Safety, a group of Patriots in New Bern, had made it difficult for the citizens to go about freely. Simple activities such as dancing and merriment were outlawed. Many of Keziah's Loyalist customers were exiled by the Committee of Safety to Canada, simply because their husbands supported the King. The war was no respecter of persons. Even children fell victim to the bloodshed. Keziah's only hope was that her husband would return to her safely.

Just then, the bell on her door chimed. Millie scampered in the door, desperately avoiding the rain. The familiar sound of military boots vibrated across the shop floor. Turning rapidly, Keziah gasped at the rain-drenched British soldier before her.

"Major Nolan!" Keziah cried as she curtseyed. "Pray tell, what brings you to New Bern?"

"My dearest Keziah, the days have turned to years, yet I have never stopped loving you!" Kissing her hand, Major Nolan knelt on bended knee, his powdered wig sullied by gunpowder and war.

"Dearest Major, you smell of battle," Keziah cried.

"Yes, my Keziah. I have returned from a victorious battle at Guilford Court House."

Weak from worry, Keziah abruptly collapsed. Major Nolan caught her and held her upright in his arms. Perched on the counter, Millie watched intently.

"Keziah! Keziah!" cried Major Nolan. "Do wake, my dear!"

Mumbling faintly, Keziah whispered, "And the wounded? What of the wounded?"

"Dear Keziah, it was a fierce battle. Governor Josiah Martin was present with General Cornwallis. The British seized the field and we reigned victorious against General Nathanael Greene's Army." Lowering his voice, he added sadly, "Though my Lieutenant Colonel Webster was mortally wounded in the melee."

"And the wounded? What of the wounded?"

"My dear, the battle was intense. The North Carolina Militia fought bravely, but they were no match for our British dragoons and Hessian soldiers. The field was strewn with dying and wounded on both sides." Keziah began to weep uncontrollably.

"Dear Keziah, I am here now. Everything will be all right." Major Nolan gently stroked Keziah's curly, brown hair, her tears soaking his tattered red jacket. "My Keziah, I must deploy to Port Wilmington and then on to York

Town. I crave your hand in marriage upon my safe and victorious return."

Standing up straight, Keziah stroked Major Nolan's face and said, "I am wed. My husband is a soldier in the North Carolina Second Regiment. Alas, he is a Patriot."

Dismayed, but understanding, Major Nolan gently replied, "I see. The wounded were taken to a nearby farmhouse. A torrential rain followed the battle. Those who did not survive were quickly buried in shallow graves."

Kissing Keziah on the forehead, Major Nolan sadly walked out the door without looking back.

Millie leapt from the counter and cradled herself in Keziah's lap, purring softly. Reaching for her Bible, Keziah read silently in the dim light, tears dropping from her face. In anguish, she prayed,

"Dear Lord, spare my husband from the cold rain! Do not leave him all alone on the field of battle…" She could not finish her prayer. The thought of losing her husband left a lump in her throat and an ache in her heart. Keziah's tears splattered in great drops onto Millie's head. The little cat twitched her ears with each teardrop, yet she remained on her mistress's lap. Her cat eyes looked solemnly into the dark night. Keziah slowly closed the Bible. Her eyes were red and swollen with grief.

Bid Farewell

Mikayla's first stop was the milliner's tent. It had wool-dyed cloth, hats, and sundry items for sale. The milliner was dressed in a colonial gown and pretty straw hat.

Picking up some gaiters, Mikayla said, "We should buy these for Santiago, to put over his shoes."

"Yeah," snorted Matthew. "It beats those plastic bags he wore in the snow! Hey, I'm going to check out the muskets and blunderbusses at the next tent."

The shop owner at the gun and iron workshop looked like he had stepped out of time. He had long hair tied back in a ponytail and a thick, woolly, grey beard. He was wearing a black three-corner hat, and Matthew thought his green breeches and tan wool tunic made him look like a Keebler Elf. Whipping out his camera, Matthew took a video of his surroundings. The fife and drum could be heard in the background as the North Carolina Second Regiment got ready to muster. Matthew reached for a replica musket, but the shop owner intervened.

"Young man, you need an adult present in order for you to handle that rifle." Mrs. McQuillan was in the park with Sweet Tea, too far away to call. The shop owner continued, "You may look, but you may not touch."

Matthew filmed the tent with his video camera. The replica rifles and blunderbusses were awesome. As he continued to film, he spotted a man standing in the shadows. The man was wearing moccasin boots and leather leggings with deer tufts embroidered along the edges. Matthew knew this film footage would be terrific for the group's project, so he zoomed in on the man. He was tall and slender, wearing a buckskin jacket with fringed edgings. Draped across his shoulder was a rifle and powder horn. His tan linen haversack was slung diagonally across his chest. The man carried a pewter water canteen, worn in a deerskin pouch strapped on his belt. Matthew thought this man was perhaps the coolest person he had ever seen! Looking up from his camera, Matthew waved. The man tipped his head in recognition, then silently continued on his way through the woods.

Meanwhile, Mikayla tried on a lace bonnet with blue satin trim in the milliner's shop. Twirling around delightedly, she asked, "How do I look?" But Matthew was long gone. There were so many beautiful costumes and so much beaded jewelry that she didn't know where to begin. Mikayla was having the time of her life shopping colonial style! The milliner, a woman wearing a simple yellow Brunswick, a three quarter length jacket with matching petticoat, approached Mikayla and showed her some of the dyed fabric in her shop.

"Mistress, may I show you some lovely wool dyed in onion skins?"

Mikayla exclaimed, "Do you mean that this beautiful orange fabric is dyed with onion skins?"

"Oh, yes. Isn't it lovely?"

Mikayla gushed, "I really like your dress!"

"Yes, Miss, but this is called my undress. All women wear an undress and my Brunswick is considered fashionable daily attire."

Mikayla giggled. "I just love your undress! May I film you and your shop?"

The milliner curtseyed and motioned her approval. Mikayla was thrilled, filming all the ceramic beaded jewelry, dresses, and hats.

She continued to film the surrounding area. Continental soldiers in blue uniforms and shiny brass buttons were in formation. All were wearing three-cornered hats and carrying muskets. Mikayla felt like she was part of the hustle and bustle. The excitement of the battle reenactment was fast approaching. In the distance, North Carolina Militia wearing tan wool tunics and plain breeches began to muster in the woods. Their simple clothing blended in the wooded forest, making them hard to see. Mikayla quickly bought her bonnet and placed a flower in it before putting it on her head. As she was about to leave, Mikayla spotted a man sitting next to his campfire, stirring food in a black cast iron kettle.

Oh, I simply must take a photo of him! she thought as she took out her phone. Besides, he was very handsome and rugged. He was impressively eating stewed meat with the edge of a knife! Around his neck was a homemade braided leather necklace with a small medallion that dangled from side to side. Just then, three little children, all dressed in pale white colonial clothes, scurried around Mikayla. Turning abruptly, she continued to film but the man was already gone.

Mike and Santiago met some British officers preparing to march. One officer, a Grenadier dressed in a tall British Bear Hat and red coat was ordering his troops to formation. They looked sharp with their shiny bayonets and scarlet uniforms. Cora met up with them and asked if she could have an interview. One gallant officer obliged.

"Yes Miss, my name is Lieutenant Colonel Webster. The 33rd Royal Foot Guards are preparing to travel along the Salisbury road for battle against Colonel Nathanael Greene."

Cora mused, *this is going to be the best project ever!*

But Hot Shot was getting restless, which worried Mike. "I think I'd better be going. Hot Shot gets jumpy at the sound of guns."

The group thanked Lt. Colonel Webster for his interview, and each took a picture with him. It was approaching 2:00. The battle would soon begin. The little group all met on the hill next to the baseball field, adjacent to the National Military Cemetery.

"What a peculiar way to watch a battle," remarked Mrs. McQuillan as she returned with Sweet Tea. They all took their seats on the bleachers as if they were watching a game.

The reenactment was splendid. The rumble of the small grasshopper cannons and muskets filled the air. Acrid smoke and dust drifted through the park. Everyone watched with anticipation as the Cavalry raced through the field with swords flashing. It was an impressive reenactment. Sweet Tea sat obediently at Cora's feet, unaffected by the gunfire. Hot Shot, however, was wriggling and tugging at his harness, clearly agitated by the event. Eventually, the battle waned and the soldiers continued with skirmishes at various locations in the park. Once the crowd had dispersed, Mrs. McQuillan reminded the children that they would meet at the pond near the bridge at 4:00.

The kids followed the crowd of people down the road, listening to the shouts and musket fire in the woods as the reenactment continued. They excitedly exchanged video clips of their adventure in the park.

"I got the coolest picture of a milliner and her pretty dress," said Mikayla. "Mrs. Nash is going to love this!"

"Yeah," said Matthew. "You could hear the fife and drum when I was in the munitions tent."

"I interviewed Lt. Colonel Webster, too!" exclaimed Cora. Even she had to admit that this kind of history was fun.

Santiago joked, "This is pretty cool. In Costa Rica we don't even have an army!"

Only Mike remained quiet. Although he loved history – especially battles – he was uncharacteristically solemn.

"What's the matter, Mike? You seem worried," said Cora as Sweet Tea walked next to Hot Shot.

"I don't know. I really can't explain it, but something's not right."

The group looked at him, perplexed, as they marched through the forest. The echo of soldiers' battle cries sounded in the distance. The crack of musket fire ricocheted through the forest. Hot Shot was getting more and more agitated, panting lightly, with little whimpers and whines.

"Maybe we should just go back," said Cora. "I think we have enough video for our project."

"Let's take a rest and see what we all filmed," suggested Santiago.

"Good idea!" exclaimed Matthew, pulling out his camera. "Check this out. This guy is so cool in his frontiersman costume – his canteen even looks authentic with a deerskin pouch! Let's see, he should be right... Wait a minute!" Matthew paused, looking at his camera. "What the heck?"

The kids all gathered around Matthew's camera. The film of the munitions shop owner was sharp and clear. They could even hear the sound of the drum and fife in the background.

"That is perfect!" cried Cora. "We can use this in our project."

"No, you don't understand," said Matthew, staring at his camera. "I saw a man dressed in buckskin clothes, an awesome rifle, and a really cool canteen! He was right here! But he's *gone*!"

"Don't worry," replied Mikayla. "I got film of a backwoodsman cooking at a campfire. We can use that instead." Searching her phone, she paused, too stunned for words. "Oh my goodness!" Everyone gathered around her phone. "I swear, y'all. I filmed the handsomest man sitting at a campfire eating stew. He was wearing a braided leather necklace with some sort of shiny pendant dangling from his neck. But, look at this."

They all watched film of three small colonial children holding hands, dancing in a circle around the campfire. Faintly heard was the lyrical chant, "Kizzy, Kizzy, find my Kizzy!" Then, the colonial children evaporated into thin air! All that was left was the black, cast iron kettle swaying from side to side.

At that moment, the sound of cannon fire ripped through the forest, sending Hot Shot into a frenzied panic. Lurching from his harness, he broke loose and ran into the woods. The kids ran after him, but he was too swift. Smoke and the smell of gunpowder gripped their lungs as they called after Hot Shot. The branches from the hemlock trees snapped and clutched at them, slowing their pace. Sweet Tea barked, sending her echo into the woods, but she remained at Cora's side. Mike was petrified of losing Hot Shot in the thick woods.

Santiago yelled out, "We've gone too far. We may get lost!" But Mike would not listen to his friends.

Cora grabbed the crumpled map from her pocket. "Mike, slow down! I think we are leaving the park!"

The woods darkened as clouds gathered into the late winter sky. Soldiers were shouting in the background, while the ripple of musket and grapeshot bounced off the trees. The sound was deafening. The smoke choked them, and fear pierced them. They were scared. No, they were more than scared; they were in the midst of war!

Catching his breath, Matthew cried, "We need to go back!"

"No!" Mike exclaimed. "I won't leave Hot Shot!" Mike began to tremble as he sunk down on a boulder.

Placing her hand on his shoulder, Mikayla whispered, "It's okay, Mike. We are all frightened."

Then a rustle in the woods stirred the branches of an old oak tree. Looking up, the kids saw a tall, slender man, wounded in the chest, his canteen dangling from his belt. His buckskin jacket was tattered and soaked, though it was not raining. He looked at them but did not speak.

Taking a woven necklace from his haversack, he placed it on an earthen mound. Stunned, the children watched in rapt silence. Then, tipping his coonskin cap, he bade them farewell.

"It's him!" whispered Mikayla and Matthew simultaneously.

A clap of thunder pierced the silence as great drops of rain descended on the ridge. Hot Shot howled long and low as he cautiously returned. Sweet Tea joined him, placing her paws on a bald patch of earth in the forest. They were all cold and drenched, standing in a huddle in the clearing.

Cora looked down as the rain-soaked ground next to Sweet Tea washed away, revealing an ancient piece of metal. The children all looked at each other. Then, Cora wiped away the red clay earth, yielding an old canteen. It was crusted with bits of deer sinew along its edge. Cora turned it in her hands, allowing the rain to wash away the mud. She could barely make out the inscription:

Mathias Sabbath Mullen NC 2nd Regiment b. July 27, 1753

"This looks like the same leather braid as the one on our pendant of Keziah LaSante," breathed Mike. They all stood in the forest as the rain turned into a downpour. Then, like five little soldiers, the war weary troop, muddy and cold, trudged along the ridge in utter silence. Cora quietly unfolded her soggy map, trying to get her bearings. No one spoke. Each was absorbed in private thoughts as they approached the National Military Cemetery.

Finally, Cora whispered, "I think I know the way back from here."

The children respectfully walked past the graves of so many fallen soldiers. Mikayla paused at a weathered grave and reached for the flower in her bonnet, placing it gently on the tomb. The four stood around the soldier's grave as Cora read the inscription aloud.

"Mathias Sabbath Mullen, North Carolina Second Regiment, Born July 27, 1753. We pay tribute to you, your family, and to all the soldiers missing in action…" Cora began to cry, unable to finish her sentence.

They all stood with tears streaming down their faces. Then, a crackle and boom broke the silence as the storm vibrated through the park.

"We'd better hurry, said Matthew. The storm will only get worse."

In the distance, they could see Mrs. McQuillan with the SUV open and ready for them to pile inside.

"Hurry, sweet peas. This storm is ugly!" Silently, the little group got into their seats. Even Sweet Tea and Hot Shot hopped into their crates without protest. "Well, I Declare! Y'all look like you've just seen a ghost!" The kids all cast a quick glance at each other.

Santiago was the first to speak. "Well, Ma'am, that's because we did."

Mrs. McQuillan looked in her rearview mirror. She pulled the car over to the side of the road.

"It's true," responded Mike in a clear and somber voice. "His name is Mathias. Mathias Sabbath Mullen of the North Carolina Second Regiment."

"We found his canteen," continued Cora, handing it to her mother. "It is braided in the same deer sinew as the pendant of Keziah LaSante." Mrs. McQuillan examined it in awe.

They all drove silently along the New Garden Highway. The asphalt roads and concrete sidewalks contrasted starkly with the past. Fast food restaurants and shopping malls replaced the wooded forest. The little group drove across Battleground Avenue as a misty grey fog rolled across the intersection. Turning, each one waved a final farewell to the Ghost of Battle Ridge.

About the Author

Susan La Serna

Susan La Serna, author and teacher lives in Raleigh, North Carolina. She was nominated for the Gilder-Lehrman American History award for Wake County Public schools in 2013. This award recognizes people who promote American History through teaching, writing and public speaking. Susan is an avid story teller, writer, and teacher. She gives book talks on historical fiction in schools and libraries. The book *Ghost of Battle Ridge* was awarded the Eric Hoffer finalist award for young readers. The story was inspired by her many years teaching US history to fifth grade students in California and North Carolina. Susan La Serna graduated from the University of California, Sacramento. She has a Bilingual Cross Cultural teaching credential. Susan and her husband Sabad have three adult children and three grandchildren who live in California and North Carolina.

www.ingramcontent.com/pod-product-compliance
Lightning Source LLC
Chambersburg PA
CBHW081330040426
42453CB00013B/2358